Pirate haiku

Bilge-Sucking Poems
Of Booty, Grog, and Wenches
For Scurvy Sea Dogs

New York Times **Bestselling Author**
Michael P. Spradlin

A **adams**media
Avon, Massachusetts

Published by
Adams Media, a division of F+W Media, Inc.
57 Littlefield Street, Avon, MA 02322. U.S.A.
www.adamsmedia.com

ISBN 10: 1-4405-0983-2
ISBN 13: 978-1-4405-0983-4
eISBN 10: 1-4405-1095-4
eISBN 13: 978-1-4405-1095-3

Printed in the United States of America.

10   9   8   7   6   5   4   3   2   1

Library of Congress Cataloging-in-Publication Data
Spradlin, Michael P.
Pirate haiku / Michael P. Spradlin.
p. cm.
ISBN-13: 978-1-4405-0983-4
ISBN-10: 1-4405-0983-2
ISBN-13: 978-1-4405-1095-3 (ebk.)
ISBN-10: 1-4405-1095-4 (ebk.)
1. Pirates—Juvenile poetry. 2. Children's poetry, American. I. Title.
PS3619.P69P57 2010
811'.6—dc22
2010027246

*This book is available at quantity discounts for bulk purchases.
For information, please call 1-800-289-0963.*

Contents

Introduction

What you hold in your hand is a piece of unparalleled history. In 1997, a small sailing vessel ran aground on an island roughly three hundred nautical miles south by southeast of Japan. While waiting for help to arrive, the shipwrecked voyagers explored the island and were shocked to discover that it had been previously inhabited by some primitive culture. When their ship was repaired, they reported the find and researchers and archeologists from around the world descended on the tiny atoll.

For years, the researchers sifted through the sands and jungles of the island, finding little of historical value. A few tools, some baskets, but it appeared the discovery would offer negligible archeological value. In 2009, the site was about to be abandoned when a graduate student uncovered a small iron box, buried in the sand inside what was thought to be a hut or other structure for the former occupants of island.

The box contained a few gold doubloons, the rusted hilt of a cutlass, and a single leather-bound journal. Researchers were shocked to discover that the journal had been written by the famous pirate One-Leg Sterling. It was one of the most valuable finds ever in the field of pirateology. Few, if any, pirates from "The Golden Age of Buccaneers" left behind written accounts, and much of what we know about the famous figures of the time is based on hearsay and oral tradition. To have the recorded thoughts of an actual pirate has given us a fascinating glimpse into his life.

What we knew of One-Leg Sterling is this: He was probably Richard Sterling, who as a young boy was stolen by pirates from his family's home near Cape Fear, North Carolina. His journal tells us his first captain was Figg, a notorious scallywag who terrorized the colonial American coast during the late seventeenth century. From there, we follow Sterling's rise through the pirate ranks until he secures his own ship, *The Black Thunder*. Aboard this ship Sterling became one of the most feared, if slightly incompetent pirates, to sail the seven seas.

Even more remarkable is how Sterling's reminiscences are recorded in the haiku form. It appears that during his time with the natives of this long-forgotten island, he was trained both in martial arts and in this Japanese poetic method.

Here, collected for the first time, are Captain One-Leg Sterling's observations of the pirate life, told in haiku form.

And don't worry about the curse of Sterling's journal. We are reasonably sure there is nothing to it . . .

PART ONE

A Pirate's Life for Me

I'm known around as

One-Leg Sterling because *I*

Only have **ONE** leg.

I also lost my

Eye in a FIGHT.   I don't have

A right   hand either.

It's *probably* a

Good thing that I'm left-handed;

Without my   right
                                          hand.

At first I **swabbed** decks.

When it comes to the ship's decks, **Pirates** are picky.

Ever *wonder* what
Pirates do on the days when

They aren't pirating?

Mostly they do LOTS

Of drinking, gambling, and *more*
Drinking and gambling.

Pirates like the dice
Except when they are loaded.

ER, THE DICE, THAT IS.

Never CHEAT pirates
If you gamble with them. They

DO NOT take it well.

You get a lot of

Promotions on pirate ships,

Due to mutinies.

My FIRST MUTINY

The captain laughed loud at me.

My sword SHUT HIM UP.

Davy Jones' locker:

A place no brave pirate fears

Until he visits.

New captain plots course

Away   from the Spanish Main.

Crack on, mateys! Arrgh!

PART TWO

Rum and Grog

DRUNK, *asleep* past dawn.

Man-o-war creeps up, unseen.

Their cannon
is LOUD.

Once an **𝕚𝕣𝕠𝕟 𝕓𝕒𝕝𝕝**

Spun from a British cannon

Found my ARSE just fine.

My arse! My Arse! *Ow!*

My arse—it burns! It burns! Ow!

I'll **KILL** those bastards!

Pirates use rum for

Many things—money, barter.

Mostly for

DRINKING.

Rum tastes really *good*.

Especially when you have

Been shot in the ARSE.

Captain says pirates

Must crack on, ARSE WOUND
or not.

His meaning is v a g u e .

Grog HANGOVERS may

Be one thing that can explain
Pirate surliness.

We don't like raiding

With *hangovers*; the SCREAMING

Gives you a headache.

Here's a *big* *secret:*

Look close at Blackbeard's
beard; you

will see **he dyes it**.

Blackbeard is *really*

Blond. But the
Pirate Blondbeard

Is not *that* scary.

There's an **old** saying
Among us pirates: "Treasure
Buried buys **NO** rum."

Actually, it's
> Not all that old, as I just

Made it up RIGHT NOW.

We do BURY rum,

So there's *always* a supply.
Today that's my job.

I really shouldn't
Hide anything when I'm **𝖉𝖗𝖚𝖓𝖐**.

Never drink and dig.

It has to be here

Somewhere on this BLASTED rock,

Or some other one.

The crew grows **angry**.

You *need* rum when hung over
And getting shot at.

SANDY BEACH mocks me.

The lost buried stash CALLS out.

THEY ALL LOOK ALIKE.

The captain **flogs** me

For losing *all* our liquor.

Flogging is NO fun.

I have to repay

In gold or *wenches* all the

Rum I   somewhere.

lost

It is hard for a

Pirate to get ahead when

He *always* owes rum.

Debt paid off *quickly.*

We RAID many ships and the

Navy is busy.

PART THREE

On the Spanish Main

If you bury our

Booty, we **KILL** some of you.

Dead men tell no tales.

If you **KILL** them all,
Who finds your treasure if you

Forget where it is?

Something you never
Forget when the pirates raid

Is all the SCREAMING.

Pirates steal because

They don't have regular jobs
With a pension plan.

Pirates don't declare

All of our *precious* loot as

Taxable income.

On my first RAID, I

Left my cutlass on the ship—

Would have been useful.

Pirates FIGHT a lot.

It's HELL on clothes. Knife slashes
And those bloodstains, too.

My ears have nO hOles.

I find earrings expensive—
At a buck an ear.

I walk with a limp

And still carry British lead
In my fleshy arse.

I've pirated years

And known just one Buccaneer.

He was from Tampa.

The merchant ships *sail*.

They're easy marks for 𝔭𝔦𝔯𝔞𝔱𝔢𝔰.

We take EVERYTHING.

Doubloon or **Ducat,**

We steal them like SCALLYWAGS.

Each makes us **rum-drunk.**

PART FOUR

Wenches

When I was eighteen

I first discovered **wenches**.

Some education.

In Jamaica I

Spent nearly **ALL** my time with

A wench name of *Belle.*

Oft' I watched her *dance*.

A dark-haired beauty, my *Belle*

Shivered me timber.

I'm no Blackbeard's Ghost!

I'M A REAL PIRATE, lassy.

Show you me cutlass?

When we sail away

My "**Jolly Roger**" won't rise.

When I pee it BURNS.

I've met fair *lasses*

Who liked the cut of my jib.

I knew not t'was CUT.

Saucy **wenches** dance.

And when I'm FULL OF RUM, they

All look beautiful.

Wenches get **ANGRY**

If you forget their name in
The morning after.

They say ALL pirates

Are CRUEL—true. But a woman

Can CUT you DEEPER.

Thought I'd *marry* once.

But don't tie us down, *lassy*

Unless we ask you.

I know pirates' *wives*

Always complain that other
Wives have better stuff.

Cap'n married once.

It didn't last. She nagged that

Blackbeard's ship's better.

Don't **like** *our* women

Mooning o'er other pirates

Like that Jack Sparrow.

Pirates are simple.

We like rum, guns, wenches. And

Women like BAD BOYS.

Glad I don't have kids.

I wouldn't want my *daughter*

Dating a *pirate*.

One night I *danced* with
One of Blackbeard's **wenches**. He
Sure does hold a **grudge**.

He got quite ANGRY.

Challenged me. I said, "KEEP HER.
SHE ISN'T MY TYPE."

We pirates keep *girls*

In every port because we

Have LOTS of down time.

If we have been at

Sea a long time, the men are

CRAZY for ladies.

Some don't even wait

Until we drop **anchor**; they
Swim to shore instead.

It's not a bad plan—

Wenches think it's *romantic*.

Tell that to the sharks.

PART FIVE

In the South Pacific

The South Pacific

Is paradise in 𝖜𝖊𝖓𝖈𝖍𝖊𝖘.

Wish we'd come sooner.

The crew is ANGRY.

Lots of **wenches**, for certain,

BUT NOT MUCH TREASURE.

We find an ISLAND.

The natives welcome us all,

Mostly the wenches.

Still wish we had some

Booty here somewhere. But the

Cap'n says, "Patience."

After a night of

Mingling with the ladies, it's

Clear. *Who needs treasure?*

Their customs are STRANGE.

Seems after sex on the beach

We are now married?

Her eyes were onyx.

Sure do wish I had known that

Her father was Chief.

Her papa caught us.

On the beach as / she CRIED. What

A **sharp spear** he has.

I TRIED TO EXPLAIN,

A pirate can't be tied down—

We tie people up.

Into the kettle

I went, CURSING whoever
Invented iron.

Natives are restless.

The **flames** lick at the kettle,

Which heats up quickly.

Her father DEMANDS

I marry her on the morn

Or I face the fire.

So here I am, **hot**

As the flames grow closer now.

Pray for sudden rain.

She is quite *angry*.

I choose FIRE over her. And she
Adds several logs.

The flames leap HIGH,
And I can't help but wonder:

Who gave them this pot?

The captain
has rum!

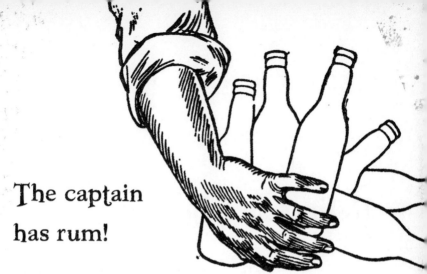

He toasts the village, and they
Drink many bottles.

Natives sleeping now.

I jump out of the kettle

And race to the ship.

Captain CURSES me.

I'm no longer the third mate,

And owe lots of rum.

PART SIX

Pirates V. Ninjas

Sail the Pacific

Looking for a place—Japan?

Never heard of it.

No land seen for days.

FOG descends like a curtain.

The sea is silent.

Captain's seen Japan.

Tells us many wild, tall tales;

Geishas and sharp swords.

The Geishas sound *good*.

I don't much enjoy sharp swords
When pointed at me.

CAPTAIN SAYS NINJAS

Are silent and quite deadly—

He's already DEAD.

Ninjas storm the ship!

We battle hand to hand, but

Their hands fight better.

One ninja finds me.

He does not **FEAR** my cutlass.

Kicks me in the face.

HOW DO THEY DO THAT?

It is almost FUN to watch.

But FACE-KICKING hurts.

They have METAL STARS.

Sharp and deadly spinners, thrown

To stick in your chest.

So much blood f$_{l_{o_{w_s}}}$ now.

Bright red where the star landed.

My shirt is RUINED.

I pull my pistol,

Point it at a ninja's chest.

Curse wet gunpowder.

(A great problem for
Many pirates: wet powder
   Due to the OCEAN.)

Somehow, I am spared.

Tied up and *thrown* in the brig.

Can ninjas *sail too?*

If there is one thing

To make a pirate ANGRY:

His own ship, stolen.

Japan is **NO** fun.

But I have learned one key thing:
DON'T SCREW WITH NINJAS.

Three days in the brig.

Never been here before now.

There are lots of **rats**.

One of them bit me

On the foot. I named him Figg,

After my first cap'n.

He sort of looks *like*

Figg did, with beady eyes and

WHISKERS; almost cute.

But he **bit me hard**.

I would KILL him gladly now

If I could catch him.

The weather worsens.

The ninjas are concerned by
The approaching storm.

They RELEASE ME from

The brig, and order me to

Take over the wheel.

At least that is what

I think they say. They talk so
fast in Japanese.

The STORM is far worse
Than any I've seen. Besides,

I'm a BAD sailor.

My captors don't know

My secret. I was NEVER

A captain. I swabbed.

But since we are all

Likely to **DIE** in this storm,

I try steering now.

Waves wash them over.

Now they scream and start sinking.

Guess ninjas can't swim.

PART SEVEN

Alone on an Island

The ship's *aground* on

The shore of this uncharted

Isle. More natives here.

My first thought is to

Wonder if they have kettles

A man can fit in.

Natives are *friendly.*

I LIVE HERE two years and learn

About the haiku.

Many times island

Women will walk up and down

A l o n g my sore back.

It sounds weirð, I know.

It's hard to describe how good

It feels when it's done.

I learn **FACE-KICKING**,

Which will come in handy when
I go back to sea.

Marines and merchants

Don't expect to get faces
Kicked when they are robbed.

One day *Black Thunder*
    Sails to my tiny island;
    Flies Jolly Roger.

As it turns out, THEY

Recently mutinied and

Need a second mate

Black Thunder's captain
Agrees to take me aboard.

It's **sad** to leave here.

I have sorely missed
The pirate's life of sailing

AND DRINKING MUCH RUM.

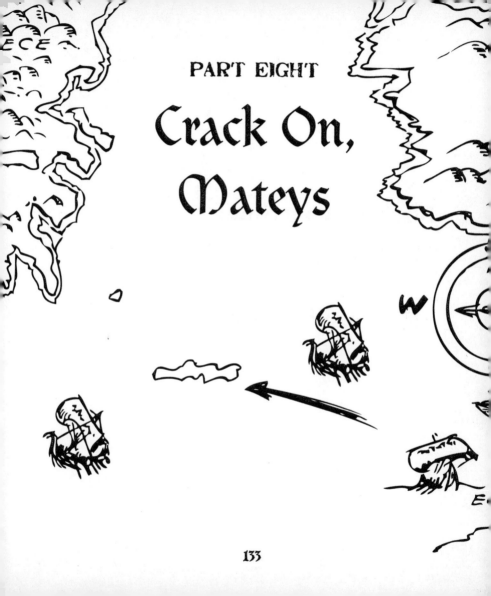

PART EIGHT

Crack On, Mateys

It takes a long time

To sail from Japan to the
Spanish Main again.

Seems not much has *changed*.

𝕿𝖍𝖊 𝕭𝖗𝖎𝖙𝖎𝖘𝖍 𝕹𝖆𝖛𝖞 is still

Here, holding a GRUDGE.

It is my first raid

Since the last time we set sail

Toward these *fair islands*.

My cutlass is **sharp**.

It should not hang on my belt.

Nearly! cut my JUNK!

Here comes the Navy.

Damn, we have no cannonballs.

Who didn't pack them?

We board their ship and

Kill all those Limey bastards

Dead as bilge water.

One sailor still lives.
Tonight we'll have some *fun* at

THE FIRE.   HE WILL NOT.

If you should be caught

By **pirates**, don't ever say

BLACKBEARD is tougher.

Unless **Blackbeard** is

The one who caught you; then it's

A good strategy.

I know **Blackbeard** well

And let me tell you, he is

Touchy about it.

𝕭𝖑𝖎𝖒𝖊𝖞, I have missed

THE SCALLYWAGS AND WENCHES;

RUM AND MY CUTLASS.

Business is *good* here.

Ships are flooding the islands.
Helps profit targets.

Captain begins to
Talk about additional
Revenue *streams*, lads.

At first, I think he

Wants us to pirate rivers,
But that is not it.

My new captain went

To *Harvard* before he was

A pirate, it seems.

I ask if *Harvard*

Is a BRITISH PRISON, and

He laughs heartily.

His idea is to

STEAL from other pirates when
They steal from others.

Sometimes I **STOLE** from OTHER PIRATES, BUT RARELY.

It leads to grudges.

I'm almost certain

There is not much **worse** than a

Pirate with a GRUDGE.

YOU TAKE THEIR BOOTY

Then it's all *revenge* this and

Blood feud that, *who cares?*

The **captain's plan** is

Not popular with the **crew**.

He goes OVERBOARD.

Now I am first mate.

I begin to think of when

𝕭𝖑𝖆𝖈𝖐 𝕿𝖍𝖚𝖓𝖉𝖊𝖗 is mine.

Then **tragedy strikes**.

Maybe not so tragic if
You don't like pirates.

We track a large ship

Not knowing it is a trick
UNTIL CANNONS FIRE.

They lower their flag

And raise the Union Jack high.

Deceiving bastards.

With their GRAPPLING HOOKS

They pull us to them and board.

This is not good, mates.

British are shocked

When you KICK THEM IN THE FACE

Many, many times.

I am fighting near
The cannons on the main deck.
There is a loud noise.

Didn't know I could *Fly* through the air, but I did. And then I passed out.

Ow. Ow. Oh dear God!

Ow. Ow. Ow. More RUM. Ow. SHIT!

Ow. Ow. Ow. More RUM!

Now I have a hook

Hand; most of my leg is gone.

THAT TOOK
LOTS OF RUM.

No eye patch but my

Eye itches. And I forget

All about the hook.

When we board British
Vessels I go first. I am

Relentless and CRUEL.

I, One-Leg Sterling

Become feared even by those

Men who have two legs.

I invent new ways

Of torturing prisoners.

IT'S DEAD RECKONING.

I'm well past the age
That most pirates retire

Or they're DEAD by now.

The *Black Thunder* is

Mine at last. Captain who once

Flogged me, died easy.

I could no longer

Take it, the constant complaints.

Overboard for him.

But Union Jack is

Everywhere we want to be.

Have I grown too old?

Not just Brits and French

American ships now too.

Think they're so hot.

I don't go on raids

And *seldom* leave my quarters

E'en for *booty* calls.

My one eye is **weak**.

The spyglass is required

To see something far.

The crew is happy.

For now, we are **rich** pirates.

NEVER trust your crew.

They would **kill** me for

Anything. I don't like how

First mate watches me.

I, One-Leg Sterling

Have raped and
                    pillaged throughout

ALL the seven seas.

WAIT, I think I might
Have miscalculated seas
When adding them up.

Sorry, I have just

Sailed on four of
them. It seems

My memory fades.

The crew drops me off
Back at the island where I
Was the happiest.

I want to tell my
Story in the haiku form
I learned here last time.

But it is **VERY**

Hard to count syllables when

You have just **ONE** hand.

Before they leave, my

Faithful crew STEALS my chest of

Treasure, SO I'M BROKE.

So the crew took my

Chest, but they don't know I took

All their rum! Ahoy!

DAILY BENDER

Want Some More?

Hit up our humor blog, The Daily Bender, to get your fill of all things funny—be it subversive, odd, offbeat, or just plain mean. The Bender editors are there to get you through the day and on your way to happy hour. Whether we're linking to the latest video that made us laugh or calling out (or bullshit on) whatever's happening, we've got what you need for a good laugh.

If you like our book, you'll love our blog. (And if you hated it, man up and tell us why.) Visit The Daily Bender for a shot of humor that'll serve you until the bartender can.

VISIT THE DAILY BENDER BLOG TODAY AT
www.adamsmedia.com/blog/humor